H

To

Recovery

Written by Anonymous

Dear reader,

This manual is a group of essays, written about the 12 Steps of Recovery as outlined in the Big Book of Alcoholics Anonymous. These essays have only one purpose, to help you, man or woman, gain a greater understanding of the twelve steps of Alcoholics Anonymous, and how they are to be implemented into your life; thus releasing you from the bondage of self-imprisonment, by alcohol, drugs, etcetera.

The manual is written in the order of the twelve steps of Alcoholics Anonymous; Step One through Step Twelve. The essays are meant to be studied, and read over, and over again; for with greater understanding, comes greater implementation into one's life.

The essays will help the new person in recovery. The essays will help the person who has been in recovery, but never fully attained the understanding and meaning behind the twelve steps. The essays will help the man or woman in recovery, who is agitated, restless, and discontented with their recovery.

Anonymous -

Step 1 - *The first action in recovery, is to identify, acknowledge, and admit that you have the disease of alcoholism. No healing can occur until one has conceded to the fact they are alcoholic, and in need of divine help, to rebuild their life.*

Anonymous' Story -

I was born in Los Angeles. The early years of my life were picture perfect. Sand-lot baseball, soccer games, surfing, and beach in the summer, nothing to predict, what was to become of my life. Lots of friends, and good grades. My parents were kind, simply, loving people. They gave me everything I needed. We were a middle class family, and alcoholism was none existent in our family history.

At the age of ten we moved from Los Angeles to Dallas. The move was traumatic for me, and I never again felt quite right. My grades slipped. My fears increased. My activities declined. I retreated into my own secluded world. By age fourteen, I had migrated too where all the outcasts go, the skate-rat club, listening to rock and roll music, and skipping school. On New Year's Eve of my fourteenth year, I got drunk. Instantly, I was released from all my fears, my stress, my anxiety. Without doubt, I thought I had found the answer to all my inside feelings, only many years later did I come to realize that it was all a lie. I covered, I masked, and I camouflaged the problems, instead of dealing with them.

With that said, all I knew, was alcohol took the pain away, it took the fear away, and fear ruled my every waking moment. I lived in fear, although I didn't know it, and that is a big part of our problem as a group, the delusion that we are like others.

I made it out of high school and entered college at Texas A & M University. There my drinking took on a whole new level. Every day, on my way home from class, I would stop by the bars, some days I didn't even get to class. I ended up failing out of college on the fourth year, just shy of completing my degree. I failed to see this as related to my drinking, but it was a direct result of it. One of the first major consequences in my life, one of many to come, but again, I could not make the connection.

This would have severed as a red flag, but after I left Texas A & M, I got a good job in the commercial real estate industry, the job masked my illness, and for the next fourteen years, I worked hard, and I drank hard. Not until the downfall of the economy in 2008, and the loss of my career, and business, did I begin to see the connection, but still my rationalization convinced me that it was not alcohol.

My drinking took on a significance after the loss of my business, which it had never done before. There was no rebounding, there was no coming up for air, or drying out this time. I drank around the clock.

I reached a bottom within months, I ran through all my finances in a year, I ruined all of my relationship, my health was in a steep decline, and even then I still couldn't stop. The power of this disease, when it has total control of a person's body, mind, and soul, is unfathomable, it becomes an insatiable monster, which never stops until you're dead. I was reduced to homeless status from upper middle class in a year, but the insanity of alcoholism still remained, I still kept drinking.

Finally in late 2009, I was put into a rehab in Southern California by my family. There, I learned of the **FATAL** nature of my disease, and that if I wanted to live, and rebuild my life, I better go to Alcoholics Anonymous. This started my journey in Alcoholics Anonymous, and I can say without a doubt, that this exploration, into my life has been by far the most healing, rejuvenating, and revitalizing action I have ever taken for myself.

The program of action is the twelve steps of Alcoholics Anonymous. The Twelve steps will help you rebuild yourself, and rebuild your life. They will mend your spirit, and heal your soul, which is the main problem of the alcoholic.

The following essays will give you an understanding, which usually takes years of accomplished study, implantation, and collaboration with those in the fellowship. If you read and re-read these essays you will find a greater understanding of what the steps mean to you, and precisely how they will help you overcome your alcoholism. These essays are only a small part of your journey, but a powerful segment of it.

Find a sponsor, get a home group, and get involved. Soon you'll realize that the best year of your life lie ahead.

Gods bless and God's speed my friends -

Anonymous -

Step 1

1. We admitted we were powerless over alcohol - that our lives had become unmanageable.

The Primary Characteristics of an Alcoholic

I was reminded of the work of Dr. Tiebout, a pioneering figure in the treatment of alcoholism. He ran a treatment facility named Blythwood. He knew, "that the characteristics of the so called typical alcoholic are, **narcissistic, egocentric, omnipotence**. The alcoholic will try to maintain the integrity of these characteristic at all costs, even though they don't believe they have them."

In a careful study of a series of cases regarding the alcoholic by Sillman, Dr. Tiebout reported that Sillman felt he could discern the outlines of a common character structure among problem drinkers, and that the best term he could find for the group of qualities was **"defiant individuality and grandiosity."**

Tiebout concurs with Sillman and states, "inwardly the alcoholic accepts no control from God or man. The alcoholic is, and must be the master of their destiny."

These character traits terminates any spiritual progress, so it is easy to see how the person possessing them has difficulty in accepting spirituality and God. **Spirituality by its mandate, removes the individual from playing God, simply by acknowledging the presence of God. This one act changes the very nature of the alcoholic.**

So, if the alcoholic can use the spiritual tools of recovery and accept the concept of the presence of a power greater than themselves, then he or she by that very step modifies presently, and possibly permanently, his or her deepest inner structure. When done so <u>without</u> resentment, anger, or resistance, then they are no longer typically alcoholic."

The Foundation of Progress

The Big Book of Alcoholics Anonymous states, "**the idea that somehow, someday the alcoholic will control and enjoy their drinking is the great obsession of every abnormal drinker. The persistence of this illusion is astonishing. Many pursue it into the gates of insanity and death.**" We learned, I through experience, that we had to fully concede to our innermost self that we are alcoholic. "The delusion that we are like other people has to be smashed."

I have learned through the program of Alcoholics Anonymous that I must admit that I am powerless over alcohol and that my life is unmanageable, while conceding to my innermost self, that I am alcoholic, and yes, I must admit complete defeat.

Once, this has been accomplished, we then have a **FOUNDATION FOR PROGRESS** in the program of Alcoholics Anonymous upon which we can build a life, a real life. A life that is measured by the love we give away.

An Admission is Required

Step One, **REQUIRES AN ADMISSION** to our innermost self that we are alcoholic. As difficult as this is to admit, I could see the progression, not only in the amount of alcohol I consumed, but also the negative effects that alcohol was having on my physical body, and my daily life.

Recovery slowly began *only* after I said, **"I am alcoholic,"** and had a desire not to drink, but that desire, (to not drink), had no power and I had to make an admission, also, that I was powerless over alcohol and that my life had become unmanageable.

In Chapter Five of the Big Book of Alcoholics Anonymous entitled, "How It Works," it states, "rarely have we seen a person fail who has thoroughly followed our path. Those who do not recover are people who cannot or will not completely give themselves to this simple program."

It is true that an admission is required. It is true that I must admit complete defeat. It is true that my life is unmanageable. It is true that I must admit to my innermost self that I am alcoholic. It is true that I must surrender to the program of AA. Once I have made these admissions and surrendered, I must integrate the program of AA into my life, in such a way, **that it becomes my life.**

Step 2

2. Came to believe that a power greater than ourselves could restore us to sanity.

Trust the Key Component of Belief

The incorporation of the steps of AA into one's life begins to break down our exaggerated egos in such a way that the concept of humility and all the benefits it can bring to our lives becomes something that we desire to have. I have learned in my experience with the program of Alcoholics Anonymous that humility is the key that unlocks the door to the Grace of God. It is only through the Grace of God that we remain sober and recovered from our character defects. Recovery from a seemingly hopeless state of mind and body. Our egos must be deflated and our desires relinquished to the will of God. Belief is necessary, but **TRUST** is essential.

Trust is the watch word of step two. We must believe that God loves us, that God wants us to be heathy, and successful. God does not want us to live in suffering. The fact was I destroyed my life through my abuse of chemicals, and my insanity associated with that abuse. God can and will change you, if you let him. Step two holds one of the greatest promises in the Big Book, that you and I can be restored to sanity.

Reliance Not Defiance

In the step Book of Alcoholics Anonymous it states, "When we encountered AA, the fallacy of our defiance was **revealed**. At no time had we asked, what's God's will was for us? Instead we had been telling God, what it ought to be. No man, could believe in God, and defy God at the same time. Belief meant **RELIANCE NOT DEFIANCE**. We saw men and women meet and transcend their pains and trials with reliance. We saw men and women accept impossible situations, seeking neither to run nor recriminate. This was not only faith, **but faith that worked under all conditions.** We soon concluded that whatever price in humility we must pay, we would pay.

Reliance upon God is the basis of the program of Alcoholics Anonymous. The Twelve Steps of Alcoholics Anonymous moves us from developing a faith in God, into trusting in God, and finally a true reliance upon God in every area of our life. This relationship with God gives us the grace and strength to transcend the trails of life, in such a way, that we are not self-centered and caught in our own needs or problems, but rather trusting in the will of God as it unfolds in our life. Freeing us to be open to the world around us, and sensitive to the needs of others.

Trust in God

There is an old Biblical story that I can relate to you, and it has to do with having **_TRUST IN GOD_**. When the Jewish people left Egypt on The Exodus, God had prepared a land for them. The Promised Land. The Promise Land was an eleven day journey from Egypt, but it took them forty years to finally enter. When they arrived Moses sent a scout from each of the twelve tribes to explore The Promised Land, and report back.

The reports came back, "the area was magnificent, a land flowing with milk and honey, but the people there are powerful and the cities well-fortified. What's more, we saw giants seven to nine feet tall." This caused **fear** in the people. The only two willing to face their fears, by **_TRUSTING IN GOD,_** were Caleb and Joshua, who were willing to enter, **_The Promised Land, anyway_**. The Jewish people decided not to enter. For the next forty years the Jewish people wandered around in the wilderness until all those who were over twenty had died. Once again they stood at entrance to **_The Promise Land_**, and only Caleb and Joshua were allowed to enter as they had been willing to face their fears by **_TRUSTING IN GOD_**.

I have had my Exodus from alcohol, but when asked to Trust in God, I could not, therefore I wandered around in the joyless, angry abyss, that is abstinence, but not recovery, for years.

Today, I face my fears by TRUSTING IN GOD, and I'm entering The Promised Land. The promised land of serenity, peace, and joy, which is recovery, not just abstinence. I came to believe, **I TRUSTED and TRUST GOD** today.

Can't Solve "The Problem" with "The Problem"

    A life lived to constantly fuel and satisfy desires, is a no win situation, it cannot be maintained; you cannot win. Our instincts are warped by fear, self-absorption, and self-seeking by everything we see around us. A life lived in defiance, self-centeredness, extreme sensitivity, and grandiosity. A life that NEVER could initiate an honest relations with other human beings. A life forever searching outside of oneself, to satisfy itself.

    This life fueled by fear and insatiable desires, became so intensely anxiety filled that I increasingly sought escape as a way to experience ease and comfort within myself. One of the forms of this escape was the increasing use of alcohol which eventually led to addiction. An addiction, I continually sought control of and increasingly found myself unable to do so. This inability to control, created a series of negative consequences in my life, driven by a self-will that knew no bounds. I continually tried to address the problem of alcohol in my life with my internal drives, **(MY MIND)**. I was trying to **SOLVE THE PROBLEM WITH THE PROBLEM.**

    I was unaware, that I have a unique disease in that it is *three fold*. I have a *physical allergy* which ensures that each and every time I put alcohol into my system I'll get sick, I'll get drunk, I'll get into all kinds of trouble, but more importantly I have a *mental obsession* which ensures that even though I don't want to drink sooner or later my mind will tell me it's ok. I'll put the alcohol into my system, I'll trigger the physical allergy and I'll get drunk again, but most important I have a **SPIRITUAL MALADY** which if not corrected, **guarantees** I will never escape the alcoholic maze, that I am stuck in.

<u>Time, after time, using my mind to create a way to control my use of alcohol and always failing to do so, has proven to me that,</u> **I CAN'T SOLVE THE PROBLEM WITH THE PROBLEM.**

The solution to our problem with alcohol and with every problem in our lives *is a relationship with God*. Only through a vital spiritual experience, tempered and enlightened by prayer and meditation, will this spiritual experience occur in our lives. Then, an only then can ***THE PROBLEM BE SOLVED.***

THE SEED IS PLANTED

There was a day I sat in a bar, dead drunk. I was fortunate that day to bump into the only person I knew who was in AA. He was eating across the restaurant, and come over to speak with me after he watched me drink my lunch. The kindness this man showed me by speaking with me was God given, he planted the seed in my mind, that my drinking was abnormal. He pointed out how others at the bar, drank one, or two, and then switched to water, or ate something. He told me I would sit here all day and night. At first I doubted what he was saying, (**Which was my disease trying to rationalize that I was okay, even thought I was on the brink of homelessness and draining my bank accounts by hundreds per day on just alcohol,**) but after this man left, I did just what he said I would do. He said I was unable to leave because I was alcoholic. I drank all night until last call. I could not deny it anymore, I had sworn to him, and I meant it, that I was leaving.

It was a year more of that insanity, until I was at rock bottom, which I had to hit, losing everything, but the good news is, you do not have to end up like I did.

Since then I've entered into AA, I have been blessed with a passion for the program of Alcoholics Anonymous which has given me a life, a real life, and I know that in order to keep this gift of sobriety, I must give it away to others. In the Big Book of Alcoholics Anonymous it says, "the entire load must be given away." It also states, "our very lives as ex-problem drinkers depends upon our constant thought of others." In the rooms, when I see a newcomer or if it is someone's first time to our home group, I will walk up to them, shake their hand and introduce myself. When anyone in AA asks for help of any kind, I give it. Generally the help they ask of is to be taking through the program of Alcoholics Anonymous, by reading the Big Book and working the 12 Steps of Alcohol Anonymous together. I always say, "yes" as perhaps this is the day they will receive the SEED, as I once did when I was blessed by kindness.

Step 3

3. Made a decision to turn our will and our lives over to the care of God *as we understood him.*

The Unique Disease

Alcoholism is a UNIQUE DISEASE in that it is **three-fold**. We have a **physical allergy** which ensures that each and every time we put alcohol into our system we'll get sick, we'll get drunk, we'll get into all kinds of trouble, but of more importance's is we have a **mental obsession** which ensures that even though we don't want to drink, sooner or later our minds will tell us its ok, we'll put the alcohol into our system, we'll trigger the physical allergy, and we'll get drunk again. The third and final component is the spiritual aspect. We have a **spiritual malady.** Our spirit is bankrupt, and until it is repaired, until our connection with God is mended there can be no sobriety. As Dr. Silkworth, the great medical benefactor of AA suggests, the thought processes of the mind of an alcoholic has to be transformed. The thought processes of the mind must undergo a **physic change**, and this change is essential for there to be any recovery.

Dr. Silkworth also states, "once a psychic change has occurred, the very same person who seemed doomed, who has so many problems, they despaired of ever solving them, is easily able to control their desire for alcohol, the only effort being he/she be required to follow a few simple rules."

The transformation of thought that is necessary to recover from a seemingly hopeless state of mind and body, occurs through the Twelve Steps of Alcoholics Anonymous. The focus of which begins in Step Three. Having admitted complete defeat, having admitted to our innermost self that we are alcoholic; understanding, "**that no human power could overcome our alcoholism**." Having begun to trust in God as a solution to our problems, we were now at Step Three. **We had decided to turn our will,** which is our thoughts**, and our life,** which is our behavior**, over to the care of God.** I knelt down on my knees and prayed The Third Step Prayer,

"God I offer myself to Thee, to build with me and to do with me as Thou wilt, relieve me of the bondage of self that I may better do Thy will. Take away from me my difficulties that victory over them will bear witness to those I would help of Thy power, Thy love and Thy way of life, may I do Thy will always."

The Operational Piece of Alcoholism

I learned in Alcoholics Anonymous that I have three basic instincts, a social, sexual, and security instinct. These instincts are God given and necessary for life, but in me I can never get enough of what it is I think I need. The great psychiatrist Sigmund Freud defines an instinct as, **a bodily need manifested in our thought process**. So what occurs for us, is our instincts manifest themselves in our thought process, and triggers our self-centered fear.

I learned in Alcoholics Anonymous, that alcohol is but a symptom of our true malady. Our true malady is self-centered fear, **afraid that we are not going to get what we want, afraid that we are going to lose what we have**.

Once our fear is triggered, we reach for our character defects in an attempt to satiate our instincts. An alcoholic can never get enough of what it is, we think, we need. Then we run around chasing our tail creating havoc in our lives, but more importantly havoc in the lives of everyone around us. This is **THE OPERATIONAL PIECE OF ALCOHOLISM**.

The solution to the problem of alcoholism is a **vital spiritual experience**, as we must give life to our relationship with God. How? By letting go of our human nature, so that our **thought process** is no longer propelled by our **instincts**, but rather by the will of God through **inspiration**.

How Will I Know God's Will for Me

I am often asked, **HOW DO I KNOW GOD'S WILL FOR ME**. The Big Book of Alcoholics Anonymous says. "That it is not probable that we are going to be inspired at all times. We might pay for this presumption in all sorts of absurd actions and ideas. Nevertheless, we find that as time passes our thinking will be more and more on the plane of inspiration." **Inspiration is defined as, "the thoughts of God implanted in the mind and soul of man."** Once the thoughts of God enters a man's soul, they are known as truth. Instantly they are right and correct.

Although I am not capable of turning my will, and my life over to the care of God in Step Three, **I am capable of making a decision, a final choice to do so.** Deciding that from this day forward, I am willing not to allow my thought process to be propelled by my human instinct, but rather by the will of God through inspiration.

If you have already made that decision **to turn you will and life over to the care of God**, may God bless you, and if you have not, perhaps now would be the time for you to decide to turn your thoughts, and behavior over to the care of God and begin to live your life in peace.

Moral Psychology

The big book Of Alcoholics Anonymous, in the chapter, "The Doctors Opinion," features, a letter given by Dr. William D. Silkworth, Medical Director of Towns Hospital. A renowned hospital in the care of alcoholism. One of the founders of AA, and the primary author of the Big Book, Bill W., was under Dr. Silkworth's care on three separate occasions in this hospital. In this letter Dr. Silkworth states "We Doctors have realized for a long time that some form of **MORAL PSYCHOLOGY** was of urgent importance to alcoholics, and that unless the alcoholic can experience an entire psychic change there is very little hope for recovery."

Dr. Silkworth and his colleagues believed that not only did the thought processes of the mind have to be transformed, but the source of what powered the thought processes of the mind had to change. The American dictionary defines psychology, as the science of the thought processes, and behavior in humans. Further, it defines moral as virtuous. Therefore the thought processes of the alcoholic had to become virtuous. **In order for this to occur the mind of the alcoholic could no longer be propelled by the human instinct or human nature, but rather by the will of God, through inspiration.**

The Real Problem

Alcoholics Anonymous, what a beautiful, beautiful program. Not only does it relieve us of our alcoholism, but the program can be applied to each and every problem in our lives.

I came to AA because, I had a desire not to drink alcohol, but couldn't stop drinking. Also, alcohol was impacting my life, specifically my mind, body, and now I know my spirit. I learned through the program of Alcoholics Anonymous that alcohol in itself was not the problem, **that alcohol was, but a symptom of the problem.** THE REAL PROBLEM was self-centered fear. **Afraid that I was not going to get what I wanted, afraid that I was going to lose what I had.**

When any of our human instincts are threatened we over-react, due to our self-centered fear, but when we make a decision, in Step Three, to turn our thoughts and our actions over to the care of God, we are really on our way to a serene and peaceful life. The integration of the remaining steps into our lives leads us to a place where we are praying and meditating on a daily basis. Praying only for the knowledge of God's will for us and the power to carry it out.

In God's hands all my problems are solved. The solution is, the **GRACE OF GOD**. May you find and find him now! In the will of God, we do not react when we perceive that our human instincts are threatened, as we are safe and serene.

Experience the Third Step Prayer

Having admitted complete defeat. Having admitted to our innermost self that we are alcoholic. Understanding that our human power could not overcome our alcoholism. Having begun to trust in God as a solution to our problems. We were now at Step Three as we had decided, to make a final choice, **to turn our will, which is our thoughts, and our life, which is our behavior** over to the care of God. Going forward we are deciding that **our thought process,** will no longer be propelled by our human instincts, but rather by the will of God.

I got down on my knees, and I prayed, "God I offer myself to Thee, to build with me and to do with me as Thou wilt. Relieve me of the bondage of self so that I may better do Thy will. Take away my difficulties so that victory over them will bear witness to those I will help of Thy power, Thy love and Thy way of life. May I do Thy will always?"

This was an important and crucial step, for the beginning of our thought process transformation, which must occur if we are to recover from a seemingly hopeless state of mind and body. However, this is only a beginning. Now that we have taken a Third Step, we must complete the remaining steps, so that the transformation of thought can be completed. We are now brought to a place where we are, **"praying only for the knowledge of Gods will for us and the power to carry it out."** We can now trust in God, not only as a solution to our alcohol use, but also as a solution to all of our problems.

The Main Problem

    The Big Book of Alcoholics Anonymous says, "what about the real alcoholic? They may start off as a moderate drinker, but at some stage of their drinking career they begin to lose all control once they start to drink. We know that while the alcoholic keeps away from the first drink, the alcoholic reacts much like others, but once the alcoholic takes into his/her system any alcohol at all, something happens, in both the bodily, and mental sense, which makes it virtually impossible to stop. The experience of any alcoholic will confirm this. **This understanding would be pointless if the alcoholic never took the FIRST DRINK, thereby, setting the terrible cycle in motion.** Therefore, THE MAIN PROBLEM with the alcoholic centers in the mind rather than in the body."

    If the problem centers in our mind, and we attempt to use our own reasoning power in an attempt to solve our problem, than we are trying to solve the problem, with the problem, our mind. This can never work, as my own experience proves. I continued to drink alcoholically even though I knew I shouldn't, and certainly did not want to.

    Lack of power, that is our dilemma and we must find a new source of power to propel our thoughts. Our thought process can no longer be propelled by our human instincts, but rather by the will of God through inspiration.

    We have found a new source of power and that is God. We have subrogated our thought process to the Will of God through inspiration. Our prayer at this moment is that anyone who suffers from the disease of alcoholism, whether actively drinking or not, may find God as the source of their power.

The Genesis

In 1930, there was an alcoholic named Roland Hazard, an Oxford Group member, who visited on more than one occasion with the noted psychiatrist, Dr. Carl Jung. After Roland had some drinking failures Dr. Jung gave to him the solution for alcoholism, which is a vital spiritual experience. **Spiritual is defined as: of or pertaining to God. Vital is defined as: life giving. So we had to give life to our experience with God and this is accomplished by surrendering our will to, the will of God.**

During this historic visit, Dr. Jung said to Roland Hazard, "you have the mind of a chronic alcoholic, and I have never seen one single case ever recover where the state of mind existed to the extent that it does in you." Roland thought the gates of hell had closed on him. He asked, "is there no exception? Yes, replied the doctor, there is. Exceptions to cases, such as yours have been occurring since early times. Here and there, once in a while alcoholics have had what are called **vital spiritual experiences**."

I illustrate these passages which are part of the chapter, "There Is A Solution," in the Big Book of Alcoholics Anonymous, so that we clearly know that the solution to our alcoholism is a **vital spiritual experience**, a **psychic change** and **THE GENESIS** of that experience is God.

If you are alcoholic and wish to recover from a seemingly hopeless state of mind, body, and spirit, then surrender your will to the will of God, and you will live in the solution to your alcoholism.

Transformation

Dr. Silkworth, the medical benefactor of AA in the letter he supplied to AA suggests that the thought processes of the alcoholic's mind, has to be **TRANSFORMED**. The letter goes on to state that this **TRANSFORMATION** of thought, must occur, and is essential if an alcoholic is to recover from a seemingly hopeless state of mind and body.

In Bill's story, Bill W. says "simple, but not easy, a price had to be paid. It meant destruction of self-centeredness as we must turn to the Father of Light who presides over us all." A clear description of the **TRANSFORMATION** of thought that must occur.

This **TRANSFORMATION** of thought was difficult for me, even though I understood that it must occur. The difficulty was that initially, I had no understanding of the power and dominance of my human nature and how all-encompassing it was. I felt a lot of fear in attempting to let go of my mind, propelled by my human instinct, as it is all that I have ever known, but it is here, at this crossroads, where I need to let go, so that the thoughts, and the grace of God **can ENTER and TRANSFORM your MIND**.

Step 4

4. Made a searching and fearless moral inventory of ourselves.

The Healing of Fear

Having admitted that I was alcoholic, **thereafter I soon found out that alcohol of itself was not my problem, that alcohol was, but the manifestation of my problem**. The real problem was **SELF-CENTERED FEAR, afraid that I was not going to get what I wanted, afraid that I was going to lose what I had**.

In the Big Book of Alcoholics Anonymous it says, "that when dealing with the fear problem or any other problem, perhaps there is a better way, as we are now on a different basis, the basis of trusting and relying upon God. We trust infinite God, rather than finite self. We are in the world to play the role God assigns. We never apologize to anyone for depending on our creator. We can laugh at those who think spirituality is the way of weakness. **The verdict of the ages is that faith means courage. All possessors of faith have courage.** They trust their God. We let God demonstrate through us what God can do. We ask God to remove our fear and direct our attention to what we should be doing. At once, we commence to outgrow fear.

Before the integration of the Twelve Steps of Alcoholics Anonymous into my life which lead to a personal relationship with God, fear haunted all of my being, in all of my moments, driving all of my decisions, in an attempt to satiate my instincts. Today, in this moment, that can change, and will change, for all of us, if we are in alignment with the will of God. If so, we will know a peace, we have never known before or experienced.

The Purpose of Step Four

The Fourth Step, is the next step in the process, **the purpose of which is to find out what is it about me that is keeping the Grace of God from entering my life**. It is through the grace of God that the healing occurs.

Many spiritual traditions include a deep and thorough look at **our past** to discover the truth about ourselves. Alcoholics Anonymous is no different.

As we work through the Fourth Step we may be getting the sense that the completed program of Alcoholics Anonymous will allow us possibly, for the first time in our lives, to live as God originally intended us to. Free of the manifestation in our behavior of, resentment, fear, and anxiety. We will then become the human beings God created us to be, and we will maximize our human potential, as the manifestation of our human nature is perfected in the will of God.

The Folly of Control

The literature of Alcoholics Anonymous says, "As alcoholics our egomania digs two disastrous pitfalls, either we insist on dominating people, or we depend upon them for too much. If we rely too much on people, they will sooner or later fail us, for they are human too, and cannot possibly meet our incessant demands." In this way our insecurity festers and grows. When we habitually try to manipulate others, to our own willful desires they revolt and resist us heavily. Then we develop hurt feelings, a sense of persecution, a compulsion to retaliate. As we redouble our efforts at control and continue to fail, our suffering becomes **acute and constant**.

We have not sought to be one in a family, to be a friend among friends, to be a worker among workers, to be a successful member of society. Always we tried to struggle to the top of the heap or to hide underneath it. This self-centered behavior blocked a partnership with anyone of those about us. Of true brotherhood we had small comprehension."

It is in the letting go of self, and trusting in God that allows us to accept others as they are and allows us to relinquish control. One of the greatest gift I have received from the program of Alcoholics Anonymous is to have true and honest relations with those around me. We can learn how to interact with others through our interaction with God in the Eleventh Step. We can learn how to love, and how to allow ourselves to be loved. We can learn not to interact with people, and personalities, which we dislike, but rather to interact with that part of them that is good, that is of God.

It is in the letting go of self, and in the trusting in God, that allows us to accept others as they are, and ourselves as we are. This permits us not only to relinquish control, but to have no need or desire to control.

Step 5

5. Admitted to God, to ourselves, and to another human being the exact nature of our wrongs.

Humility with Serenity

      The Fourth Step is the beginning of a process in which we listed our resentments, fears, harms, and sexual conduct on a four column inventory to determine the exact nature of our wrongs. Step Five is "admitted to God, to ourselves, and to another human being the exact nature of our wrongs. In many great spiritual traditions a deep introspective period is necessary, and Alcoholics Anonymous is no different. The purpose of which is to discover within ourselves what it is about ourselves, that is keeping the grace of God from our lives, and then a **confession. Our Fifth Step**. Where a sense of relief from the shame and guilt of our past life is released. If we are to overcome our alcoholism than a review and admission of our defects is necessary.

      The chapter, "<u>Into Action,</u>" in the Big Book of Alcoholics Anonymous states, "We shall be more reconciled with discussing ourselves with another person, when we see why we should do so. The best reason first. Time after time newcomers have tried to keep to themselves certain facts about their lives. Trying to avoid the humbling experience, they tried easier methods. Almost invariably they got drunk. Having persevered with the rest of the program, they wondered why they fell. We think the reason is they never completed their housecleaning. They took inventory alright, but held onto the worst items in stock."

      All the steps of Alcoholics Anonymous are humbling, but none more so than the Fourth and Fifth Step. To tell someone the deepest darkest side of ourselves is a very humbling experience, but along with that comes a sense of relief. For many, this is the first time in their lives, they are free from, shame, guilt, and remorse of their past. There is a sense of serenity. The Step Book of Alcoholics Anonymous says. "When **HUMILITY** is combined with

SERENITY a great moment is apt to occur," and for me it was the presence of God in my life. If we are willing to do a complete Fourth Step as outlined in the Big Book of Alcoholics Anonymous followed by a complete and honest Fifth Step, than **HUMILITY** will intersect, with **SERENITY** and we will know a peace that we have never before experienced.

Humility as a Recovery Tool

The basis of all the AA's Steps is **HUMILITY.** The spirit of humility is necessary as our egos must be deflated in order to achieve long term **SOBRIETY**.

To be clear, (1) admitting to our innermost self that we are alcoholic, (2) learning to trust in God, and (3) making a decision to turn our will and our lives over to the care of God, were all steps on the road to humility.

In the Fourth Step, identifying who we are, and acceptance of those facts, were certainly ego deflating and humbling, but for me, the biggest step in accepting humility, **although not the last**, was the Fifth Step, where I shared my Fourth Step list, the deepest darkest sides of myself with God, and another human being.

Another step in humility occurs as we go out into the world of our wreckage (**OUR PAST**) and make our amends. Reconciling the wrongs we have done in the past, and finally the Eleventh Step, where a **recovered alcoholic resides**, as we are praying only for the knowledge of God's will for us and the power to carry that out. Only a man or woman filled with a humble spirit can exist in the eleventh step.

It is humility which unlocks the door to the Grace of God, and only through a humble spirit may we recover from a seemingly hopeless state of mind and body. **Humility is indispensable**.

A Fifth Step Story

Having shared the Fifth Step with myself and another human being, having exhibited a sense of humility, having acquired a clarity of mind and a sense of peace, I was emboldened to complete the final piece of the Fifth Step. That is **to admit to God the exact nature of my wrongs.**

I met my sponsor at a small chapel, and initially I was fine, until he swung open the doors to the chapel and I looked down the center aisle. I became immediately aware of the stillness that existed within this hallow ground, but not in me. I froze for a moment and swallowed hard. I fully realized that in the next few moments I would experience the most profound events I had ever participated in. In this time and in this moment, I was to seek the forgiveness of God, for all I had done wrong in the past.

Yes, it is a special experience to feel the nearness of God and to share that with another. It is an experience that is not meant to be missed. A complete cleansing of the past, a sense of forgiveness and a clean slate and a new start on life, and most important a new relationship with God.

Step 6 & 7

6. Were entirely ready to have God remove all these defects of character.

7. Humbly asked Him to remove our shortcomings.

Am I Entirely Ready

As an alcoholic it is difficult for me to give up control, as I want to apply some sort of cognitive therapy, or behavioral modification as an effort to control my defects. For me this is like applying a band aid to a festering infection. Control of our defects is not the issue, but rather that these human defects are not to exist in our behavior at all, as it is our defects that are keeping us from the perfection that God seeks in us. When we are in the will of God, our human character defects, which exist in our nature, cannot possibly manifest themselves in our behavior.

I am willing to have God remove all these defects of character? That is the real question.

Giving

In the book, <u>Alcoholics Anonymous Comes of Age</u>, the historic visit to Bill W. by his boarding school chum Ebby T., is a true miracle. Ebby T. came to share with Bill what had happened for him, and too him. **HOW HE GOT SOBER**. He outlined the precepts of the Oxford Group, **(WHICH LATER BECAME AA's TWELVE STEPS,)** one of which applies to humility. He said, I was told to practice **GIVING**, the **GIVING** of myself to somebody else.

I have learned that it is humility, which unlocks the door to the Grace of God. In order to grow in humility, I must begin to let go of my selfish-desires, and begin to practice faith in God, which eventually blossoms into complete trust in God. Trust in God initially is difficult as my whole life I have used my instincts and my intellect to propel myself thought life. When I was faced with a self-imposed crisis that I could not overcome with my human power, I had to find a higher power. As the Big Book says, "I trust infinite God rather than finite self."

To surrender. To trust in God. One must lead a life of caring for others. This was not possible in me before. Today, and only through the Grace of God, am I able to place the needs of others ahead of my own. I am able to **GIVE** of myself to others.

An alcoholic who is humble enough to trust in God, knows that the **GIVING** of one's self, for the helping of others, is the fulfillment of the Twelve Steps of Alcoholics Anonymous.

THE BASIC INGREDIENT

Having completed Steps One through Five, there are some fundamental recovery questions in the Big Book of Alcoholics Anonymous that we must answer before we can move on.

1) Have we omitted anything (Step 4)

2) Is our work solid so far (the step work)

3) Are the stones,(*the Steps*), properly in place, as we are building an arch, in which to walk through a free person

4) Have we skipped, in the cement we put into the foundation (*our effort in working the Steps*)

If we can answer these questions in the affirmative, than we have completed the first five steps in such a way that we have acquired the humility necessary to be entirely ready to have God remove all these defects of character.

The Big Book of Alcoholics Anonymous states, "If we can answer to our satisfaction, we then look at Step Six. We have emphasized willingness as being indispensable. **Are we NOW READY to let God remove from us all the things we have admitted are objectionable**?" If we can answer yes, we have completed Step Six.

The Seventh Step of Alcoholics Anonymous is, "**Humbly asked Him to remove our shortcomings**." In the Step Book of Alcoholics Anonymous it says, "this lack of anchorage to any permanent values, this blindness to the true purpose of ourselves produced another bad result, for just as long as we were convinced that we could live exclusively by our own individual strength and intelligence, for just that long; was a working faith in a higher power impossible. This was true even though we believed God existed. As long as we placed self-reliance first, a genuine reliance upon a higher power was out of the question. **THE BASIC INGREDIENT** of all humility is, a desire to seek and do God's will."

    I have learned through experience that belief in God is not enough, that I must trust in God in every area of my life, even as my everyday life unfolds. The purpose of the program of Alcoholics Anonymous is to bring me from a thought process that is propelled by my human desires, to a thought process that is propelled by the will of God. In the will of God my defects although they exist in my human nature, can't possibly be manifested in my behavior. It is only through true humility, a desire to seek and do God's will, that behavior modification to this extent can occur. **Free your-self from the bondage of self, trust in God in all things, and you are protected from your disease of alcoholism.**

The Root of the Problem

It is my experience with my character defects, that when I can recognize them and set boundaries, I'm doing nothing more than applying a band aid to a wound that is in need of stiches.

The reality is I have to get at **THE ROOT OF THE PROBLEM**. My character defects exist in my human nature, they do not exist in the will of God for me, (**Humility**). Therefore if I am willing to perform the work necessary for the spirit to be awakened in me, and to live in the back half of the Eleventh Step, which is, "praying only for the knowledge of God's will for us and the power to carry it out." Then the root of the problem will have been addressed.

In Alcoholics Anonymous there is a well-used saying which is "let go, and let God." **The let go part is, that we will no-longer allow our thought process to be propelled by our human instinct, and the let God part is, going forward with God, practicing HUMILITY.** The will propelled through inspiration is the key. As this transformation occurs THE ROOT OF THE PROBLEM is healed.

Become the Being God Created

When I first walked through the doors of Alcoholics Anonymous I had no idea what to expect. Quickly, I was able to see what worked for others, **a belief in and dependence upon God**. As Bill W. once said, "would I have it? Of course I would."

The Sixth Step of Alcoholics Anonymous is, "**were entirely ready to have God remove all these defects of character**." I have learned through the program of AA that alcohol is but a symptom of my true malady. My true malady is self-centered fear. **Afraid that I am not going to get what I want, afraid that I am going to lose what I have**. Once my fear is triggered, I reach for my character defects in an attempt to satiate my instinct. The dictionary defines, defect, as the lack of something necessary for completion, or perfection. (***In our case a lake of proportion, our defects are never satisfied***.)

I learned in the Fourth Step that I needed to find out what is it about me that is keeping the Grace of God from my life. It is there that I discovered the exact nature of my wrongs, **as I made a list of my character defects**. In the Fifth Step I confessed my character defects. Now in the Sixth Step I am entirely ready and willing to have these character defects removed.

Again, it is my character defects that are keeping me from the perfection of God, from **BECOMING THE BEING GOD CREATED** me to be, instead of a person that is self-centered and selfish who cares only for his/her desires and what they think they need in life. A person who is willing to use almost any means necessary to fulfill their human desires, but when we turn from the desires of our human instinct, and become obedient to the will of God, we are now living in harmony with our creators will for us.

Step 8 & 9

8. Made a list of all we had harmed and became willing to make amends to them all.

9. Made direct amends to such people whenever possible, except when to do so would injure them or other.

Another Chance to Pray for, and to Forgive

As I began working with the four column inventory of my Fourth Step, my resentments, fears, harms, and sexual conduct, my sponsor suggested that I begin to pray for, and to forgive all those on my lists.

The Eighth Step is, "**made a list of all persons we had harmed and became willing to make amends to them all,**" is **ANOTHER CHANCE TO PRAY FOR, AND TO FORGIVE** all those on my lists, and to begin doing the same with new situations which may arise. We are already in possession of an Eighth Step list extracted from our Fourth Step inventory. As we begin to pray for, and to forgive all, I am making a beginning on Steps Eleven and Twelve.

Prayer and forgiveness are essential tools if we are to recover from a seemingly hopeless state of mind and body. We learned in the Fourth Step, that resentments toward others is the number one offender to a relationship with God, as we are called to love all, (**the one exception is that we are never accepting of evil, or those that practice evil deeds, you will know these instances, and people immediately, as you are now in a new state of being.**)

The Eighth Step provides for us, **ANOTHER CHANCE TO PRAY FOR, AND TO FORGIVE** all those on our lists, which is necessary to bring the Spirit to our Ninth Step amends.

Motivation to Complete Step Nine

The Big Book of Alcoholics Anonymous says, "we have a list of all persons we have harmed and to whom we are willing to make amends. Now we go out to our fellows and repair the damage done in our past. We attempt to sweep away the debris that has accumulated out of our effort to live on self-will, and run the show ourselves. If we haven't the will to do so, we ask God until it comes," (the ninth step prayer).

"Remember, it was agreed upon at the beginning that we would go to any lengths for victory over alcohol."

Now, here I am at Step Nine, and it is somewhat daunting task, but easier as now I have the experience of, and a connection with God on my side. The Fifth Step brought a sense of relief, the beginning of a serene life, I felt the presence of God in my life, but Step Nine, now opens up a whole new world to us, it reconnects us with our fellows as never before, and gives us the ability to look ourselves and the world in the eye again. It is here that we are re-born.

I learned through the program of Alcoholics Anonymous, not to consider any harm others had done to me, as I was praying for, and forgiving those on my list. In the Big Book it states, "under no condition do we criticize such a person or argue. Simply we tell them that we will never get over our drinking until we do our utmost to straighten out the past. We are there to sweep off our side of the street realizing that nothing worthwhile can be accomplished until we do so, never trying to tell them what they must do."

This is how I approached the Ninth Step. I began with my immediate family. The irony of many of my amends is that life doesn't occur the way we would want it too. Many of the amends I had to make were impossible because the other party was deceased and he passed on long before I had any consciousness that I owed amends to them. So I went to their grave, and there grieved over what had happened.

To those I could not see, and to those that did not want to see me, I sent a sincere and complete letter and prayed for the best for them. It really did become easier as I moved through the list. **In the Fifth Step, I began to feel serenity, and now with the Ninth Step task complete, I had extricated myself, through the grace of God, from the past and I was free - maybe for the first time in my life.**

Step 10

10. Continued to take personal inventory and when we were wrong promptly admitted it.

Admit and Accept

In the Step Book it says, and this is paraphrased, a continuous look back at our liabilities and a real desire to grow, by this means, are necessities for us. We alcoholics have learned this the hard way. More experienced people of course, in all times and places, have practiced unsparing self-survey and criticism of themselves. For the wise have always known that no one can make much of one's life until self-searching, becomes a regular habit.

Through my daily inventory, I can now **ADMIT AND ACCEPT** that my character defects are a part of my human nature. I have come to understand that my human nature is defected, and I must accept this about myself.

Self-Centeredness

When I become angry and resentful, it is in that moment, that I manifest my human **SELF-CENTEREDNESS**. In the Big Book of Alcoholics Anonymous it says, "**that we think this is the root of our troubles**." It also goes onto say, "it is plain to see, that a life which includes deep resentment leads only to futility and unhappiness. To the precise extent that we permit these do we squander the hours that might have been worthwhile. But with the alcoholic whose hope is the maintenance and growth of a spiritual experience, this business of resentment is infinitely grave. We found it fatal. For when harboring such thoughts we cut ourselves off from the sunlight of the spirit."

The solution to our alcoholism is a vital spiritual experience. We must give life to our relationship with God. We accomplish this by turning from our human nature and living in the will of God. We receive God's will through inspiration conditioned by prayer and meditation. We can't possibly be in the **Will of God when we are manifesting our SELF-CENTEREDNESS** in our lives.

Powerlessness Understood

So much has been accomplished and a good portion of the program of Alcoholics Anonymous has been completed, but now the personal relationship with and the dependence on God takes on a much deeper and all-embracing meaning.

In the Big Book of Alcoholics Anonymous, in the chapter, "How It Works," it says, "we are in the world to play the role God assigns." I have learned through the program of Alcoholics Anonymous that this may be accomplished through the practice of all the Twelve Steps and specifically by integrating Step Eleven into my life, **BUT** it is in the **TENTH STEP**, through daily examination of my life, **that we uncover that our character defects continue to manifest themselves in our behavior, even though this reaction to life is not what we want.**

It is here, in the conflict of not wanting to manifest my character defects in my behavior, that I am thrown back into Step One, and I can now see clearly that I am not only **POWERLESS** over my use of alcohol, but **POWERLESS** over every other aspect of my human existence. I had previously learned that all my life must be given to the care and direction of God, but now through experience, I perceive this with more clarity, and at a much deeper level.

It is in the taking of first a daily inventory which eventually expands into all our waking moments. **We then begin to fully understand the pervasiveness of our character defects, encoded into our human nature.** To overcome the manifestation of our character defects in our behavior, we must give-up our human nature (**OUR SELF-CENTEREDNESS**) to, and must abandon ourselves utterly to God, for it is in the infinite power and love of God that we are healed.

Discovery through Inventory

    My experience has taught me the value of the daily inventory, and all that can be discovered and transformed as we move away from the instincts of our human nature, and progress into the world of the spirit.

    I have realized there is no need to wait until the end of the day, as we can address the manifestation of our defects as they occur. The Step Book of Alcoholics Anonymous says, "there is the spot check inventory taken at any time of the day that we find ourselves getting scrambled up." I find the spot check inventory to be invaluable. It may be as simple as identifying unkind thoughts that we may have of people who are not like us in appearance, or beliefs. If we can identify it as it is happening, we should not wait until the end of the day to address it.

    When we have completed the first Nine Step of the program of Alcoholics Anonymous we have extricated ourselves from our past. Now we are free of the shame and guilt we carried for years. By implementing the daily inventory and then eventually moving into the spot check inventory, we can now deal with the manifestation of our character defects as they occur in the present, so that in this moment, and at this time we are free of the instincts of our human nature and one with God.

    We have dealt with and released our past. **DISCOVERY THROUGH INVENTORY** is a tool of recovery available for us. It helps us too, **not to create another unpleasant past** that is carried by us into the present. Now we are truly free of the bondage of self, and at peace in the will of God.

No Need to Create A Past

The program of Alcoholics Anonymous has in place the apparatus necessary to deal with our character defects as they surface, either in the daily inventory, or the spot check inventory. If needed, I can use the Ninth Step which is, "made direct amends to such people wherever possible, except when to do so would injure them or others." If we are aware of our trespass, than amends are necessary, than we go ahead immediately and make the amends in an effort to live in the present, in the will of God, and not to create a past, that we will have to remove ourselves from later.

If our actions cause us to have any shame or guilt than we use the Fifth Step of Alcoholic Anonymous which is, "**admitted to God, to ourselves and to another human being the exact nature of our wrongs**," so that we may be living in the present with a clean slate and a tranquil mind.

If we are willing to take inventory, to make amends, and share our wrongs with God, ourselves and another human being. There will be, **NO NEED TO CREATE A NEW PAST**. This allows us to live in the **present**, in the will of God.

As alcoholics we worked hard to free ourselves from our past, and if we are willing to integrate the program of Alcoholics Anonymous into our lives in such a way that it becomes our life, **than the creation of a negative past, that at least subconsciously is having a negative effect on the present, will not occur. THIS IS AN IMPORTANT TOOL OF RECOVERY.**

Another Way to Look At Step Ten

I like to visualize the Tenth Step as a hallway that I must walk down in order to come into the room where I can live with God. This hallway has fallen into disrepair, and consequently needs mending. The ceiling is leaking, there are holes in the walls, and the floor is buckled. Fortunately the program of Alcoholics Anonymous has given us an instructional manual on how to repair and remodel the hallway.

We should incorporate the Tenth Step inventory initially into our daily life and eventually into all of our waking moments. We must be persistent. **Persistence is enjoying the time between the promise of God, and the providence of God.** The implementation of Step Ten will revolutionize your life. It will create harmony with you and your environment.

(Family, work, friends, institutions, etc.)

If you fail to implement this in you daily life you will begin to feel the pull of your character defects, you will begin to build a new unpleasant past, you character defects will gain strength, and chaos will begin again in your life.

Step 11

11. Sought through prayer and meditation to improve our conscious contact with God *as we understood Him*, praying on for knowledge of His will for us and the power to carry that out.

To Know Peace

    The big book of Alcoholics Anonymous says, "either God is or He isn't, either God is everything or He is nothing. **What is our choice to be?**" When we come to the point in our recovery where we have no desire to turn back to our old life, but we are fearful of letting go of our human nature and living in the will of God, it is at this precise point that the above statement has to be answered.

    I may have answered in the affirmative earlier in my recovery, but it is only now, that I understand what is being required of me. If I am to be free of manifesting my human defects, if I am to live a life where I am tolerant of all, but never accepting of evil, to live a life free of fear, anxiety, and anger, to be respected and loved, to have a spirit of charity and forgiveness, to know joy. Then I'm utilizing Step Eleven to its fullest extent, and I'm living in the will of God.

Conscious Contact

CONSCIOUS CONTACT is a personal relationship with God. In this precise moment, and at this time. I do not look back, and I do not look forward, as I live in contact with God in the present. Through the Grace of God, in this moment, I have let go of my human nature, as my instincts are no longer propelling my thoughts, but rather my thought process is propelled by the Will of God.

The Big Book of Alcoholics Anonymous says, "we may face indecision. We might not be able to determine which course to take. Here we ask God for inspiration, an intuitive thought or decision. We relax and take it easy, we don't struggle. We are often surprised how the right answers will come after we have tried this for a while. What used to be the hunch or the occasional inspiration gradually becomes a working part of the mind. We find our thinking, as time passes, will be more and more on the plane of inspiration. We come to rely upon it."

The back half of the Eleventh Step says, "praying only for knowledge of God's will for us and the power to carry that out," as my human nature will never do the will of God in an absolute way. It is here that a recovered alcoholic lives, in the will of God, through a **CONSCIOUS CONTACT**.

I Don't Know if it's a Good Thing, or a Bad Thing

Many centuries ago there was a kingdom, and in this kingdom lived a farmer, and this farmer had a beautiful white stallion. The king of the kingdom desired the farmer's beautiful white stallion and sent an emissary to the farmer, and offered the farmer a quarter of the king's kingdom for the beautiful white stallion. The farmer said, "no, as I love my beautiful white stallion." The very next day the beautiful white stallion run away.

Soon all the people from the village came running out to the farmer and said, "what a bad thing that happened to you, as you could have had a quarter of the kings kingdom, and now your beautiful white stallion has run away."

The farmer said, **"I don't know if it's a good thing, I don't know if it's a bad thing**, all I know, is my beautiful white stallion has run away." The very next day the farmer is out working in the field, and he looks up on the hill and what does he see? He sees his beautiful white stallion, and behind his beautiful white stallion are four whiter stallions, just as beautiful as his."

So all the people from the village came running out to the farmer and said, "that's a good thing that you didn't trade your beautiful white stallion for a quarter of the kings kingdom, as now you have five beautiful white stallions you could probably get half of the kings kingdom."

The farmer, he says, "**I don't know if it's a good thing, I don't know if it's a bad thing**, all I know, is I have five beautiful white stallions."

The very next day the farmer's son is breaking one of the wild white stallions in, and is thrown from the stallion, and breaks his leg.

So all the people from the village come running out to the farmer, and they say, "that's a bad thing that happened to you. You need your son to work in the fields, and now he can't, as he has a broken leg."

The farmer, he says, "**I don't know if it's a good thing, I don't know if it's a bad thing**, all I know is my son has a broken leg."

The very next day the kingdom goes to war, and all the able bodied men are being drafted into the army, and they are going to the front, but the farmer's son can't go, as he has a broken leg.

The moral of the story is: **that we are not to JUDGE what is occurring in our lives as good or bad, but to trust in God praying only for knowledge of His will for us and the power to carry it out.**

Step 12

12. Having had a spiritual awakening as the result of these steps, we tried to carry this message to alcoholics, and to practice these principals in all our affairs.

Serenity

I have committed myself to the Twelve Steps of Alcoholics Anonymous, as I have realized that the program of AA must come first in my life, and along with that comes a personal relationship with God that allows me to have the opportunity of a life full of **SERENITY,** regardless of what is occurring in that life.

The Step Book of Alcoholics Anonymous says it so well. "We are no longer frightened and purposeless. The moment we catch even a glimpse of God's will, the moment we begin to see justice, and love, as the everlasting truths in life, we are no longer disturbed by all the seeming evidence to the contrary that surrounds us in purely human affairs. We know that God lovingly watches over all of us.

Integrating the Twelve Steps of Alcoholics Anonymous into our lives and manifesting the principles of that in our behavior produces the opportunity to have a serene life, peaceful purposeful, and joyful.

Can't Give Away that, Which you Don't Have

The TWELFTH STEP of Alcoholics Anonymous is, "**having had a spiritual awakening as a result of these steps, we tried to carry this message to alcoholics and practice these principles in all our affairs**."

This step clearly places a responsibility upon me, as **I CAN'T GIVE AWAY THAT, WHICH I DON'T HAVE**. The Big Book of Alcoholics Anonymous says, "we have received the power to help others." The power to help others **is a result of the spiritual awakening received in the TWELFTH STEP**, and until that has occurred for us, it is going to be pretty difficult, for that to occur for another alcoholic that we may be helping.

Once the spirit has been awakened, we are asked to carry this message, not only through words, but also by incorporating the principles of Alcoholics Anonymous into our lives, so that our behavior can become an example for others.

An Awakened Life

I have admitted complete defeat. I am trusting in God. I have made a decision for my thought process to be propelled by the will of God. I have asked God to remove from me anything objectionable. I have made my amends. I have learned through the program of Alcoholics Anonymous to pray and meditate daily. Through the Grace of God I am living in God's will in this moment, today, and I am a living example of the power of integrating into our lives the program of Alcoholics Anonymous.

This occurs for all in whom the spirit has been awakened. Once the spirit has been awakened in us, we are than given the power to help others. We are to carry the message to others, not only through words, but more importantly through our behavior.

Having been given the power to help others, it is a wondrous thing to see others live **AN AWAKENED LIFE**, to become awakened also. We experience fulfillment in our own lives, as we watch others recover, to become loving, and giving human beings.

Sponsorship

I have had the privilege of working with many people in Alcoholics Anonymous. I have worked with all walks of life, rich and poor, young and old, believers and non-believers, Christians, Jews, and Muslims. I do the same thing with everyone. I always have the Big Book of Alcoholics Anonymous between them and me. I simply open the book and we begin reading at the preface. As we read the book, we discuss the material. I don't change anything for anyone. **The solution, a vital spiritual experience is the solution regardless of what their problem may be, who they are, race, wealth, sex, etc.**

(Obviously if someone has mental, or medical issues, additional help is necessary for them. I never tell anyone what they must do on these issues, and I urge you to leave that to the professionals.)

Just follow the material, and help them incorporate the Twelve Steps into their lives as you move through the pages. A practice that can be replicated by anyone, and repeated endlessly. You are not to be a banker, doctor, nurse, lawyer, etc.

I know that my behavior is being observed. Not just whether I can talk, the talk, but more importantly, can I walk, the walk. Am I practicing the principles of AA? In the forward of the book, **The Twelve And Twelve**, it says "the Twelve Steps are a group of principles, spiritual in nature, which if practiced as a way of life can expel the obsession to drink and enable the sufferer to become happily and usefully whole."

The following is what they see in me, I am responsible. When asked to take someone through the book of Alcoholics Anonymous, I say yes. I never consider whether I have enough time. I simply just make it work. There isn't a greater exercise one can participate, than to help another recover from a seemingly hopeless state of mind and body. We meet once a week for an hour. My emotional state rarely, if ever changes one week to the next, as I am serene, and at peace. I never prepare for a meeting with a new man or woman, as I am dependent upon and trusting in God.

The Resentment Prayer

I found that in compiling my Fourth Step Resentment list, the best way to deal with **RESENTMENT** was to pray for, and forgive those on my list. In the Big Book of Alcoholics Anonymous chapter, "How It works," it states, "we realized that the people who had wronged us were perhaps spiritually sick. Though we did not like their symptoms, and the way they disturbed us, they like ourselves, were sick too. We ask God to show us the same tolerance, pity, and patience we would grant a sick friend. When a person offended us, we said to ourselves, perhaps this is a sick person - how can I be helpful to them? God save me from being angry, thy will be done. God will show us how to take a kind and tolerant view of each and every one."

As an Alcoholic, we find that RESENTMENT is the number one offender to a peaceful and serene life. If we are to lead an Alcohol - free - life, we must let go of **RESENTMENT**, and there seems no way possible without the help of God.

A Purpose Beyond Ourselves

     Early on I heard, "I wouldn't trade my worst day in AA, for my best day when I was out there." I was skeptical of these proclamations, but the member's sincerity, could not be questioned, as these people were just like me, in that, we all suffered from an illness, but they no longer had the struggle I did. More importantly they seemed to be living an enjoyable and fulfilling life. The other obvious characteristics they had were openness and giving, as they seemed to have found a purpose beyond themselves in Alcoholics Anonymous.

     Integrating the program of Alcoholics Anonymous into our lives in such a way that it becomes our life, takes us out of ourselves, and gives us the power to help others. That we become capable of putting **others needs before our own**, is a direct result of the healing that occurs for us, **and it is a miracle**. We know that we have found a purpose in our problem, by helping others who are just like us, to recover from their alcoholism, and in so doing, we are fulfilling **A PURPOSE BEYOND OURSELVES.**

My hope for you - is that you may begin this course of action, and continue to seek, until you find GOD. All miracles are possible with God.

May God bless on your journey.

Applying the Twelve Steps to any problem in your life

The Twelve Steps of Alcoholics Anonymous can be applied to all issues you are having in your life. The Twelve Steps of Alcoholics Anonymous can be applied to any addiction you may afflicted with, not Just Alcohol. Drugs, sex, eating, personal relationships, working relationships, family, etc.

Here is a brief tutorial of how the application works.
- I'm having issues with my boss at work.

1. I'm powerless over my boss at work, and for that fact all other people in my life. I want to be right and other to follow my every order, and they do not, this is making my emotional state unmanageable, my boss isn't listing to me.
2. I believe that a power greater than myself can return my thoughts to sanity.
3. Turning back to God and letting his inspiration show me the right actions here. What would the Lord do?
4. Writing the issues down and FINDING MY PART in these issue. My character defects, with my boss.
5. Admitting my part in this problem. To another, whom I trust, and then admitting my fault's to God.
6. Believe that these character defects can be taken away.
7. Asking them to be taken away, so I can return to my normal, balanced self, and life.

8. Knowing my part, my issue with my boss, I now know I need to make an amends, for my part in the disharmony.
9. Making the amends to my boss never discussing his/her defects in this amends.

You are now returned to sanity and harmony in your life. Your side of the street is clean, work life will return to balance. This is how the Twelve Steps can be incorporated into ever aspect of one's life, and work, for the total benefit of you and everyone around you.

With your help, we can bring our loved ones back from the brink of self-imposed destruction. They can begin again, on a solid foundation. They will start out on a new path, towards a new horizon, on a fresh journey to recreate their live.

This Volume is but a stepping stone in understanding of how one transforms themselves and their lives into a new way of living, into a new mind set. All suffers of alcohol and drug abuse, etc., will need without a doubt a self-help organization, a fellowship, such as Alcoholics Anonymous, etc., to which they can assimilate into, and become part of.

IT is ESSENTIAL, that the afflicted one has a fellowship. No long term recovery can exist without it.

God bless and God's speed

-Anonymous

If these essays have helped you, please recommend this text to those who are in need of help, to rebuild their lives.

The manual can be located at www.amazon.com

Search for: Road to Recovery, Volume 1

Thank you and God bless you

- Anonymous